THE DATA DOODLE DASH

DEDICATION & LEGAL MUMBO JUMBO

To anybody who was ever called a Geek (they didn't know it was our superpower).

This book wouldn't be possible without my amazing supportive husband, mum, dad and crazy kids.

ISBN 978-1-7638388-0-2 (paperback edition)

https://learn-to-data.com

WELCOME DATA EXPLORER

To a world of data fun,
where you explore visuals,
one by one.

From A TO Z with doodles galore,
we'll uncover the secrets DATA'S
got in store.

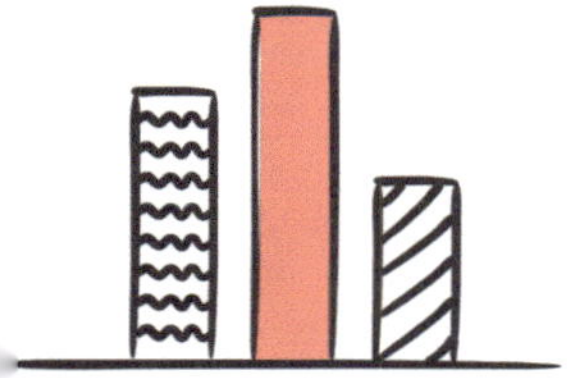

A AVERAGE

A is for
Average,
where numbers
meet

B

BAR CHART

B is for

Bar Chart,

where groups

compete

C COLUMN CHART

C is for
Column Chart,
standing tall
and neat

D DASHBOARD

D is for
Dashboard,
a visual treat

E EXCEL

E is for **Excel**,
where numbers
march to the
beat

F

FLOW CHART

F is for

flow chart,

with processes

we repeat

G

GAUGE

G is for
Gauge,
measuring
the heat

H HEATMAP

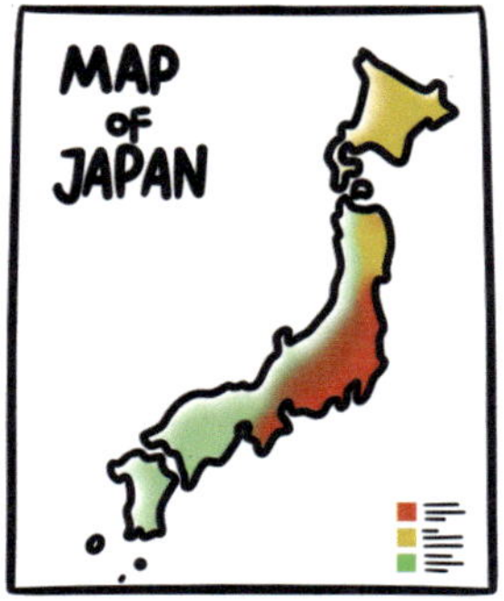

H is for
Heatmap,
a colourful
array

Oh no, you forgot to rhyme !! !!

I INSIGHTS

I is for

Insights,

that show us

the way

J JITTER PLOT

J is for
Jitter Plot,
where dots
group to play

K KPI

K is for **KPIs**,
tracking goals
every single
day

L LINE CHART

L is for
Line Chart,
with trends
that fly away

M METRIC

M is for
Metric,
Key data to
know

N NUMBERS

1 2 3

4 5 6

7 8 9

N is for
Numbers,
neat in a row

O OUTLIERS

O is for
Outliers,
that break from
the flow

P PIE CHART

P is for
Pie Chart,
with slices
on show

Q

QUARTER

Q is for

Quarter,

one fourth of

the dough

R REPORT

R is for
Report,
to share
insights and
ratios

S SCATTER PLOT

S is for
Scatter Plot,
dots high and
low

T TREE MAP

T is for
Tree Map,
piling blocks
like cargo

U

UPDATE

U is for

update,

where new

data will show

V

VISUAL

V is for

Visual,

that makes

your data glow

W WAFFLE CHART

W is for
Waffle Chart,
colouring rows
like a pro

X AXIS

X is for

X-Axis,

showing how high the data can go

Y YEAR ON YEAR (YOY)

Y is for

YOY,

comparing the

past

Z ZONES

Z is for
Zones
and that's
the last

SO FAREWELL, DATA EXPLORER, TILL WE MEET AGAIN,

May your data adventures continue till then

MORE BOOKS OF DATA JUST AROUND THE BEND,

AN AUSTRALIAN DATA STORY

FROM A TO Z

A JAPANESE DATA STORY

A DINO DATA STORY

Made in the USA
Monee, IL
05 November 2026

67383294R00019